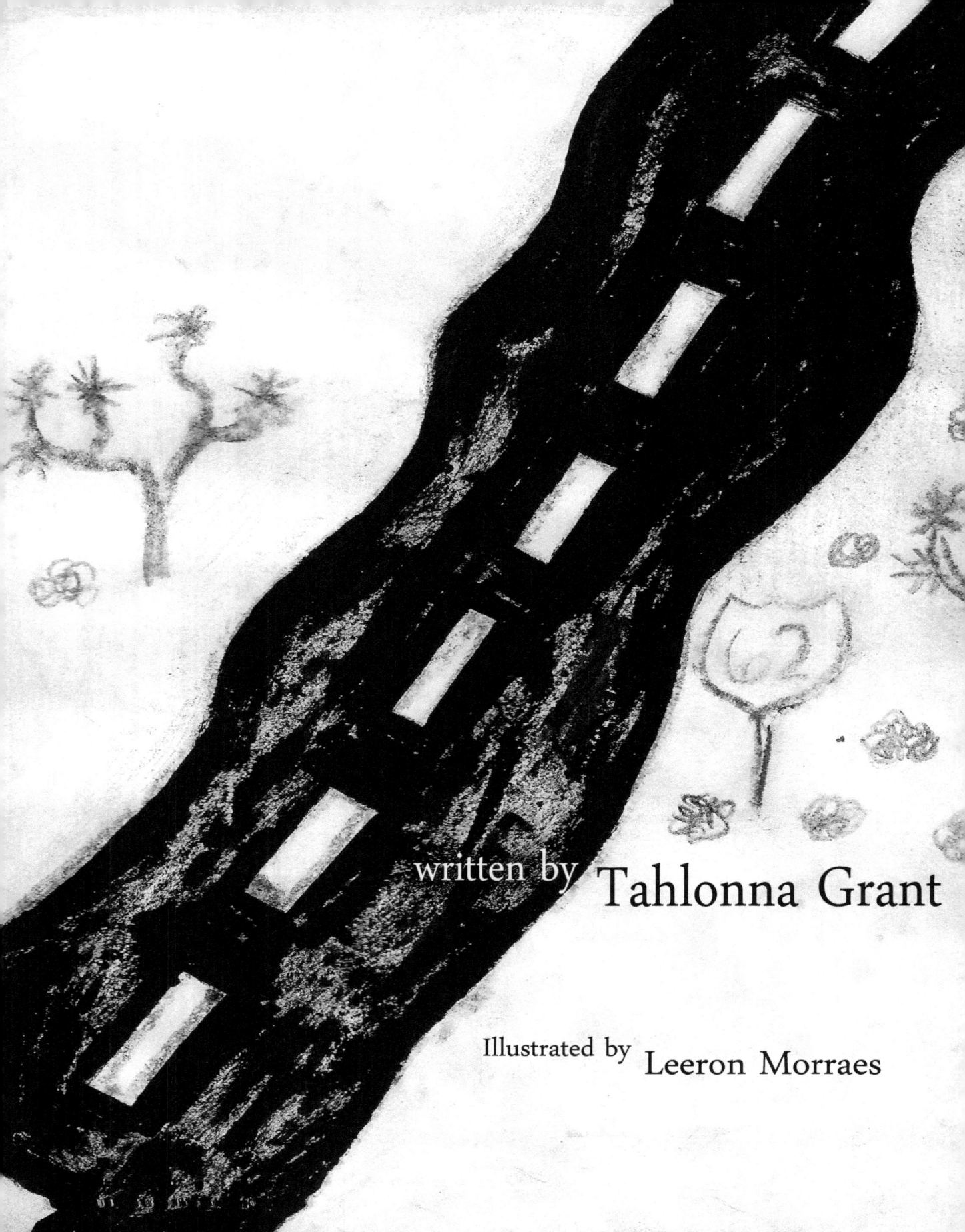

written by Tahlonna Grant

Illustrated by Leeron Morraes

WRITTEN BY TAHLONNA GRANT

ILLUSTRATED BY LEERON MORRAES

ISBN: 978-1-950471-05-8

ISBN 10: 1-950471-05-5

No part of this book may be reproduced or transmitted in any form or by any means, electronic or mechanical, including photo-copying, recording, or by any information storage or retrieval system, without permission in writing from the author, illustrator, or publisher. www.beansproutbooks.com

for those that wish upon a star...

The Road.

The Road.

What does it all mean?

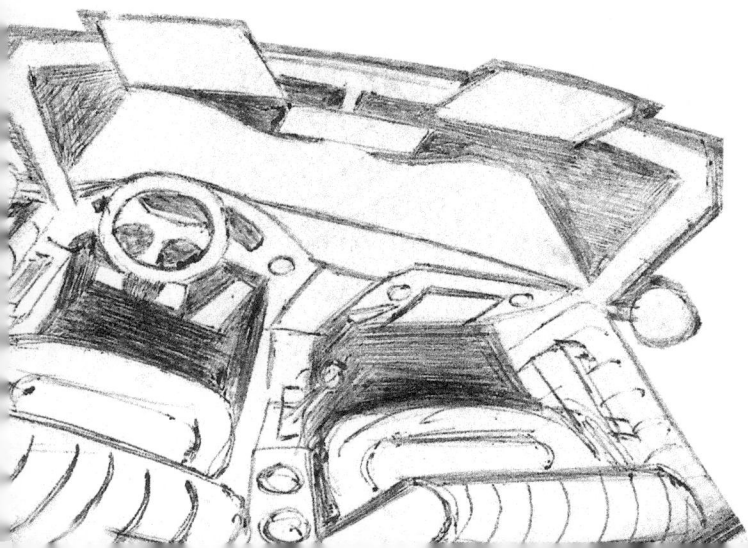

A husband in Queens hugs his expectant wife

A woman on the lower Westside primps for a dinner date

IN Brooklyn, a man sits on a chair and wonders

"Where did the time go?"

A Morongo Winter's Night

The smell of wood-burning fireplaces

The Christmas tree light off in the distant desert

The cool night air below a million and a half stars

A Morongo Winter Night

The Red Balloon

The red balloon buoyed over the hot clay roof in the Mohave desert. The little girl watched the balloon play in the wind from her window. She wondered how the tiny string could fight the wind from launching into the heavens.

Suddenly and unexpectedly, the red balloon floated high-high-higher, until it was surpassing the clouds and making its escape from the confines of the hot clay roof.

Had she caused the balloon to succumb to the wind just by the sheer power of thought and wonder? She sure did wonder.

That Night

"It's a blackout."

The winds whipped outside in the hot humid night air that was the Joshua Tree desert. The cars on nearby Highway 62 became louder, suddenly sounding like crashing waves beating into the ocean crashing against each other. Like a jet plane or space rocket taking off all wind against machine all the time.

Full of Sky

A star full of sky

A lightbeam

A star that looks like a car

Bright nose facing upward with its doors open

A real star like a car

What if stars are vehicles?

To drive around the Galaxy the universe

The Neverending Sparkler

Once upon a time, a star was born! It shined so pretty and bright on that wondrous winter night. The star's mom gave it a name to match its beauty and brightness just the same. Hence, the neverending Sparkler was born on that cold December morn!

If you ever want to see, just spin around and say, "Twinkle, Twinkle" and it will begin to show its neverending glow.

Stardust is what you'll be able to see, sprinkling down on you and letting you know that tonight was meant to be!

The End

Morongo Valley

On 3 acres right off of Twenty-nine Palms Highway sits our little tannish-brown ranch house in the desert. Mountains and hills surround with ice capped in the distance. Most of our days are spent cooking and eating --- today was my legendary roasted chicken with fresh local carrots, asparagus, onions, cilantro, and lemon. Stirring the golden broth that juices from the chicken no matter where you go on the planet makes it feel a little more like home.

Goodnight Morongo Valley

Morongo Valley

A little town

A hamlet

With lots of trees

Situated high up in the mountains

With lots of leaves

A pretty place with

Lots of open space

Come peek and take a look

It's like a place out of a

Storybook

Goodnight Joshua Tree

At night, the wind sounds
like waves crashing into the ocean

The mountains stay the same
Most without a name
Here long after we leave
for another lane,
And part ways with this Earth,
They will still be here wide as ever
in girth.

Joshua Tree, it feels like one of the places where the
Earth
gave birth,

Goodnight Joshua Tree.

NEW YORK

A note about New York...

Le Struggle: Writing NY's Perfect Poem
Originally written on Christmas Day 2015 2:13 pm

Raggles couldn't put his finger on New York and neither can I. Writing a poem about New York is how do I say: difficult... a tad bit it is. Even making you write grammatically incorrect sentences with a handwriting not of your choice out of sheer annoyance and aggravation that you can't quite get it right. Can't quite put a finger on it.

New York, who wants to be a cliche? Or give just facts? Or tell a story that is typical? In a city of so many contrasts, why is finding one unique thing so difficult?

A girl in Washington Heights
sits on the steps
A lady on the Upper Eastside
takes her terrier for a trot
A man in a Brooklyn loft
paints his first masterpiece
A boy in Little Italy forms
meatballs at the
family restaurant

Watching

from the

Empire State Building

Waiting

to cross the

Brooklyn Bridge

Wanting

To move back to

Manhattan

Wishing for better days

Exciting city

Bustling full of crowds

The city with the most people

in its 300 square miles

Nine million people call New York City

their home

Some live in Queens, Staten Island, Brooklyn,
the Bronx, Manhattan

or alone

To get home some cross water by ferry or foot

Or ride under it in tunnels

Goodnight New York

It's Halloween night
The whole city is dressed
And ready for a fright
The subways get busy
Half past eight
And people rush off
At the Greenwich stop
Tunnels spout them out
Into the street parade
of masked revelers
It's Halloween night
The whole city is dressed
And ready for a
Sight
A girl stands to the
side
in her
peacock mask
of bright green purple
and blue
all alone
head cocked
A man dressed
Like a baby pushes
A stroller through
The dark loud parade
It's Halloween night

HE

The rickety gold jeep raced through rows of careful cactus lining the deserted Mojave highway on both sides, the pink sun fading farther into the distance. He sped away in the lingering burgundy light, moon time rapidly approaching. He felt alone amongst the watchful gaze of the dark, Goliath-like mountains pointing with their curious peaks.

Las Vegas

Greatly enriched and empowered they'd been as the first to adulterate the landscape (literally) with glitzy buildings filled with liquor and shows and, of course, gambling --- the casino aspect was a big deal. Big money! Win Big! Loosest slots in town! Signs beckoned drivers and passersby on foot to come in and try their luck at spinning to win.

Many got suckered in, others didn't. Once an old man with a cowboy hat and boots was walking out of a gas station and someone asked him if he gambled to which he responded with an emphatic 'NO' and went on to say in a rural accent, "Vegas wasn't built on winners!" and walked away with a fat butt ensconced in tight-blue wrangler jeans.

Residents who stay up
Late at night
Middle of the Mojave
Desert that is
Hot, dry, and tough
This desert can get rough
But when the machines jingle
The people tingle--ch-ching!
yet wonder why
their pockets are so dry
'Take a spin, you're sure to win'
The casino man prods
So the people stay and play
Gaming their lives away

Goodnight Las Vegas

City of late nights and lights
Dancing in the Desert

City in the Middle of the Mohave
Known as the Party Place in an otherwise quiet state

City that almost never was
Until someone in the 'Biz
Took a risk
On an arid place
Where living things could barely habitate

The people all rushed in
Hoping to win a huge fortune
The machines began to jingle
Making the people tingle
And forget about
How they missed home so much.

The residents stayed up late
at night
in this all-night city
in the desert called
Mojave

A tiny, dusty desert town
Adorned with lights
The strip glows
Green and gold
Begging you to spin
And hope you win

L.A.

L.A.
its something that allures
Me to this city
But, what is it?

Los Angeles
The city of angels
But, is it really?
When everyone has an angle?

Nine million people
all crammed
into one bowl
trying to eat cereal together

But is it enough?
is there enough?
is there ever enough?
For everyone to thrive
And not just survive
For surely there has to be
Enough there
For you and me

So let us go
into the abyss
that is the hills
LA, always so bright
And bushy-tailed
scooping them all up
in her green smoggy bosom

Untitled

We were a family.. it was weird..
I could write..
A book about that week
So anyway we were a family
for that time at least.

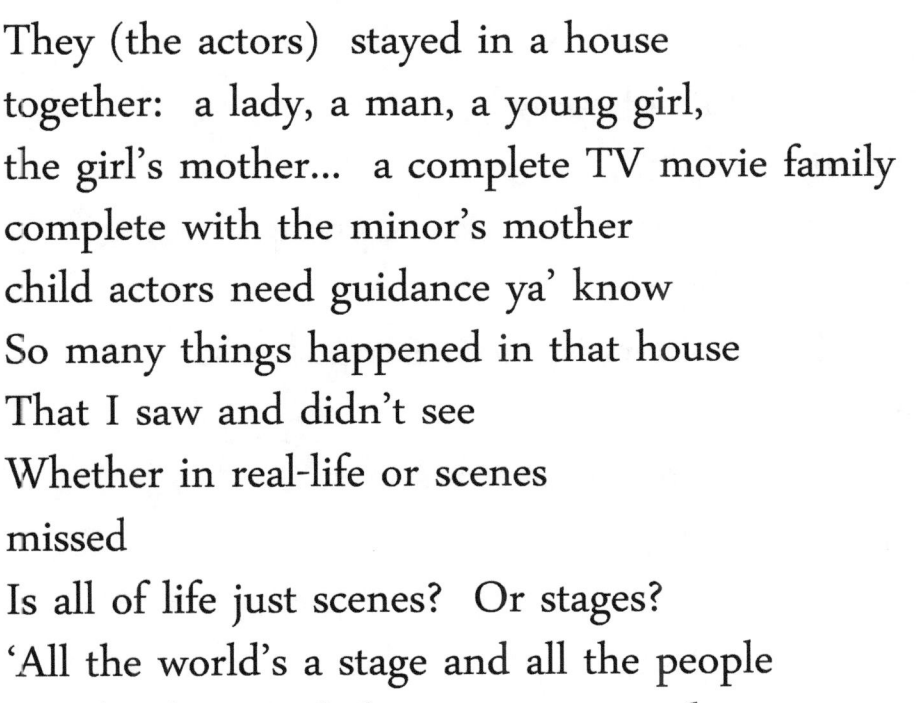

They (the actors) stayed in a house
together: a lady, a man, a young girl,
the girl's mother... a complete TV movie family
complete with the minor's mother
child actors need guidance ya' know
So many things happened in that house
That I saw and didn't see
Whether in real-life or scenes
missed
Is all of life just scenes? Or stages?
'All the world's a stage and all the people
merely players' Shakespeare once said

An unlikely family
One brunette, a bright young redhead (or ginger
as she liked to call herself) and some more physical
descriptions that I wont bore you with
So we were a family

Us
them
Became one
With strangers we'd never met
The hot desert sun shined
Through at 122 degrees
Las Vegas a red terra cotta
roofed house with rocks for grass as
the setting
A house in the middle of sprawl
But still felt alive
inside because of the many fine actors giving
performances of their lives
Right inside of that otherwise nondescript house
So focused
I peek through the door to see if a scene
is going on and if I may enter

Silhouettes are what I see
The bright desert sun at its hottest and brightest
mid day blares though the tan-colored everything
house as the actors move slowly about towards their marks

Sunny clear slow-walking ghosts
are what they look like from outside through the blinds
Nope, can't go in yet
Middle of a scene
I tell myself
It is 114 and the sun
is burning my shoulders
arms legs every part
exposed

I must wait outside anyway, I reconcile
with myself
I don't know at the time
but I will be getting to know these
actors and crew pretty well
This is my first movie
well really my second
The first one was such a short, BS thing
it really didn't count
So I guess my first legit real movie
As a producer, I did ok
I'll take the reins more
When I write-direct
that'll be when

This train is starting to
roll faster and faster
just like I predicted
Keep up with it a
and outrun it and
you'll be a star
I watched her do what she does
Create an amazing actress out of an
ordinary person
She worked night and day in that
sad, lonely house... but she's probably
going to make it... make it big...
Run the city..city of LA her home today to
play...far away is she from Las Ve...Vegas that is where
she shot this flick
The one in which we all
became a temporary family
and had a ball
Gay parties, gun ranges
You name it
We did it all big or tall
and had to call
Las Vegas the desert our home a fake place
to create an imaginary family
Was everyone pretending?
Or were they actually real?

You never really know with actors
They can take a toll
Or be the one to help let you go
let go of fake notions
that being unhappy's the way
that sacrificing feeling alive
is worth pseudo financial stability
that we have any other choice
but to live life at 200 miles
an hour
that life is actually waiting
for us and our stupid job that we hate
and not just passing us by
and trade security for vitality for really
living it
that dream whatever it is

Those actors
These artists
Reminded me of that
and all of this
And what I wanted
And why I moved out here
An why not just go for it...that dream..
the one deferred
Because remember what happens to a dream deferred?

He winded the cold curvy beach roads
with Bean Noodle beach on the left.

They had memories there...of
fields of flowers and child's play,
skipping along old railroad tracks
while etching their names above
the cliffs that dropped into a
deep ocean that had taken
many especially the curious ones
who wanted to see a little
more than...

The night
is young, but
are we still?

The night is
dark do we
buy into it?

The night is
young, but are we
still?

Night for her means
she can't stay

So she runs and goes
To another place
hoping for a better day

Goodnight Fort Lauderdale

Diamonds on the water
  Parasailing over
    Bountiful breakfasts
    Las Olas

Sweet skies over Sunrise Way
Morning light brightens
Millionaires' Row

Momyer Falls

The stream leads to a cloud

The stream leads to a cloud

Leaves blanketing the ground

And crunching like fresh snow

beneath your feet

Oak Glen full of apple orchards

The place of dreams and fairytales

Fresh cider and jelly

Special apples

u-Pick your poison

Orchards abound

Goodnight San Francisco

San Fran
A city that's pretty
Chocked full of redwood trees
And skyscrapers alike
Competing based on height.

Towering trees
A real sight to see
A wonderful bouquet to breathe
Spicy, sweet, whispering notes of bark
Seems like you can hear them speak.
As you walk among them, they try to talk.

But, what about the famous fog?
A real sight to see
The atmosphere loves her
  like no other
A fog that hogs
The hole of a city.

It can be quite nice
when it rolls in every night
Creating a city that's cozy

as you are sitting at
A sidewalk cafe and
you are reminded of your day
and
smile.

The Splendid Sun

The sun is warm on the window
The trees are still within their compartments
The bird flies high over the vista
First North, then at the last minute change
Change of mind
Change of directions
West he goes instead
At once
The bush blows ever so slightly
in the quiet desert oasis breeze
Mountains open their arms out wide
The bird appears again
Or maybe its another
This time higher
Flying high
Sailing his wings
Snow bubbles and peaks
Atop the mountain
Like whipped cream on a chocolate
Sundae
The bird flies by
Again
Sailing in circles
Maybe he is just...

Enjoying the day?
With no clear cut place
to go
Sort of like me
At this moment
Watching the cars and birds
go by
As the sun
The splendid sun
Warms my arms

A Letter to a Goldfish

Gold fishy-Fishy in the sea
Are you grabbing that plankton or do you
really just want to see me?

Fishy oh Fishy
What do you want to be?
A doctor, a lawyer, or
Something even more important?

Under so much pressure
Little Fishy I see
Because mommy + daddy are pushing
You in so many directions
you may not want to be

Little Fishy make sure you
Listen
Now don't you give up
So many people may
want you to hear
instead of speak
from your heart
Your little fishy heart
The truth of all truths
For you know what to do
What's right for you
Block it all out and plug
Your ears with more water
Tell them not to Bother
With their Thises and that's
No's to your Yes
Let them know
the truth
That you know
Best

The Pearl

A precious, beautiful pearl
lies in your harbor
It glistens and floats
Eluding capture
Iridescent sparkling white
Buoying in the blue
    Ocean
Deep in the sea
A sea that matches the sky
The pearl
Wonderful pearl
Still eludes their capture
And smile at the bottom of the ocean
Sparkle remaining hidden in the shell
Pearl of a Lifetime
Never to be held.

WE

Wandering,
Searching,
Longing...
Hoping...
Wanting...
Needing
Finding

The Human Experience

the stars stared at her unblinkingly from their perch high above the mountaintops.

the night was dark as
a jet train and the
stars adorned the deep sky
like millions of diamonds,
precious and rare as
the night they were
party to or a part of

Goodnight Hong Kong

Pearl of the Orient
Your night lights sparkle
Along Victoria Harbour
Red lanterns hang
Wishes of wealth, health, happiness and luck
It's Chinese New Year!

Lions and dragons gyrate
in the streets
Bright, colorful costumes of red and gold
Parade floats dance by
It's Chinese New Year!

Tasty dumplings and noodles are noshed
Drums and cymbals bang
Celebrations for many days
Red envelopes are given
"Hongbao!" scream the excited children
It's Chinese New Year!

The Road

New Mexico still

609 am

Out of nowhere in the midst of deep conversation a bunny rabbit jumps out of the middle and happily frolicks full speed towards our car- - nevermind it's i40 and we're going 80.

"Did you see that?" she asked.
"Yah a bunny rabbit!"
"I saw it," he smiled with a knowing glance.
"Are you half bunny rabbit or something?" she asked and wondered to him.
Because bunny rabbits and jackalopes always seem to appear around you.
He laughed, "No I just like bunny rabbits…"

As she waits the camera
fades out
As he watches the night
gets darker
What's the point? she thinks
Whose it all for? she
wonders
Why are we here?
What are we waiting for?! she demands
Life.
Dreams.
Love.
Happiness.
Dreams.
Some have em'
Some lose em'
Dreams,
Some keep em'
Some like to delete em'
But, what happens to a dream lost?

Does it sit there and grow frost?
Really, what is the
true cost?
of a dream lost?
Do we pay the ultimate cost?

For not seeing it through to
The end when greatness could
be right around the bend.
Greatness
To be great
It's what we all want
Greatness
We strive for as
Soon as we learn to walk
And talk
We battle others,
When just being kind would get
us closer to the finish line.

The Night

It is so cold at night
But the wind still speaks
It is so very cold at night
But the wind still howls
For why does she frown?
Why not just take a bow?
She spins, she twirls,
But what a world
to give her a whirl
yes, the world whirls
us around
As a dancer does his partner
Spinning and grinning
Looking to win it
Win it all
Ah, to win it all!
Oh, but what a ball!
A ball it would be!
to win
Not just for you
but for me
Hmm...what will she do?

A face without
a place in this society
But its supposed to be
for you and me
You and me, too, she says
Come my way and
we will go to
a place you don't know
Take my hand
and you'll see, she says
It's a place
for you and me...

about the author

If you are reading this, you picked up my book. And you opened it. And turned some pages to get here. For that, I thank you. My greatest joy is sharing my poetry and stories with people just like you.

Tahlonna Grant is a writer, educator, and publisher. She is the author of Goodnight the Book and The Adventures of Scooter and Lima Bean series.

For more please visit
www.beansproutbooks.com

ANOTHER
www.ANOtHERgraphicnovel.com

www.ingramcontent.com/pod-product-compliance
Lightning Source LLC
Chambersburg PA
CBHW060506240426
43661CB00007B/931